Science Close-Up®
VOLCANIC ROCKS

Written by Robert Bell
Illustrated by James Spence

A GOLDEN BOOK • NEW YORK
Western Publishing Company, Inc., Racine, Wisconsin 53404

The Swelling Mountain

In the early spring of 1980, an earthquake shook Mount Saint Helens.

It was a small earthquake. Nobody would have paid much attention, except for one thing—Mount Saint Helens is a volcano. It had been inactive for over 120 years. But in the case of a volcano, no one takes chances.

When scientists came to Washington State to study Mount Saint Helens, they recorded more earthquakes, as many as 50 a day. Then the volcano started to erupt, and a hole, called a crater, opened in its top. Clouds and smoke rose up from the crater. The mountain was like a kettle of water starting to boil.

Then scientists learned that the mountain was swelling up, like a balloon filling with air. But it wasn't air. It was magma—molten rock at more than 2000°F, almost 10 times hotter than boiling water.

The Mountain Explodes!

Two months after that first small earthquake, Mount Saint Helens blew up!

People as far as 5 miles away were killed by the heat and force of the blast or buried under the ash and hot mud. Almost 60 people and countless wild animals died.

The blast was heard 180 miles away. It blew about 1,300 feet (about as tall as the Empire State Building) of the mountain's top into pieces. Millions of trees were knocked down. The cloud of smoke and steam rose more than 12 miles high and scattered ash for hundreds of miles. Ninety miles away in Yakima, Washington, ash lay 3 to 4 inches deep in the streets.

What Is a Volcano?

The surface of the Earth, called the crust, is solid. The temperature beneath the crust is so hot that rock actually melts. This molten rock is called magma.

A volcano is a place where magma rises upward through cracks in the crust. As the magma rises, it forces open a passageway to the surface called a chimney.

magma chamber

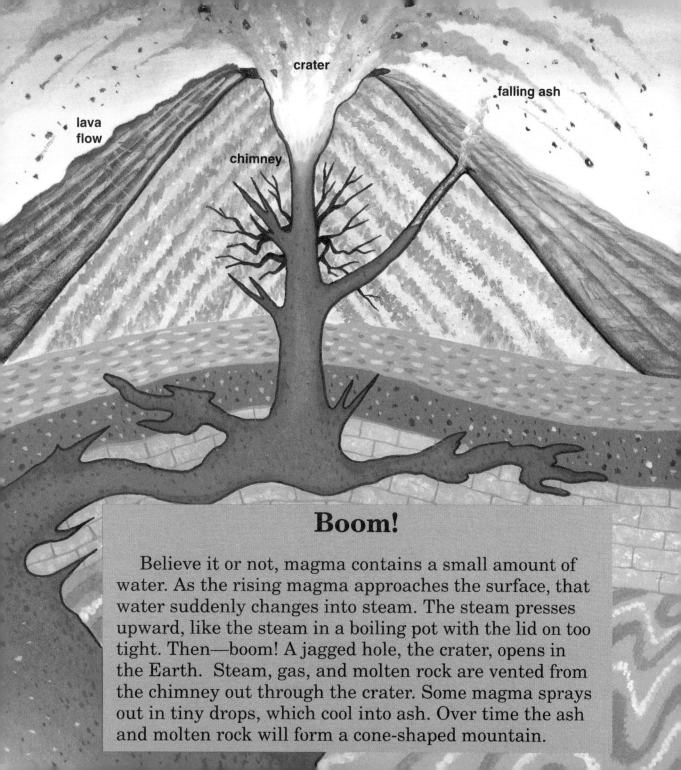

crater

falling ash

lava flow

chimney

Boom!

Believe it or not, magma contains a small amount of water. As the rising magma approaches the surface, that water suddenly changes into steam. The steam presses upward, like the steam in a boiling pot with the lid on too tight. Then—boom! A jagged hole, the crater, opens in the Earth. Steam, gas, and molten rock are vented from the chimney out through the crater. Some magma sprays out in tiny drops, which cool into ash. Over time the ash and molten rock will form a cone-shaped mountain.

Flying Blocks

The eruption may also shatter part of the mountaintop and fling pieces of solid rock through the air. These pieces are called blocks. When an old volcano such as Mount Saint Helens explodes, jagged blocks may be sent flying thousands of feet.

Pumice

After the blocks have been cast out, many volcanoes next eject a rock so light that it floats.

This rock is called **pumice**. To understand how pumice is formed, imagine that an erupting volcano is like a bottle of soda being opened. As the bottle cap is loosened, a hissing sound is heard and bubbles form on the soda. The hissing is like the steam escaping from the volcano.

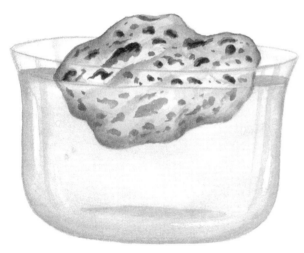

pumice rock floating

froth from soda

The steam creates bubbles, too. The top of the magma is like the froth of bubbles on the top of soda.

The erupting volcano throws this molten froth high in the air. Suddenly it cools and becomes solid. The inside of each bubble becomes a hole and the thin walls of the bubbles become stone.

Bombs

After the bubbling froth has shot from the volcano, bigger pieces of magma called bombs may erupt. Bombs usually become oval or round in flight. They fly through the air like glowing cannonballs.

Sometimes bombs twist into ropelike shapes. If they have time to cool and grow solid in the air, they keep their shape. But if they are still molten when they hit the ground, they flatten out like thick pancakes.

scoria

cutaway view
of variegated
interior of scoria

Scoria

Finally the magma may flow out of the crater like a fiery river. It starts as bubbling streams that harden into a rock called **scoria**. Scoria is full of bubbles like pumice, but it is heavier and usually darker in color. Scoria often contains chunks of hard, glassy rock as well.

Thick Magma and Rhyolite

Not all magma is the same. Some is thick and hardly flows at all. Volcanoes with the thickest magma make the biggest bang when they erupt.

Why? Because thick, gummy magma is hard to move. Bubbles of steam take longer to break free. There's time for more water to change into steam. And the more steam, the bigger the explosion.

measuring
temperatures
of lava

Once it reaches the Earth's surface, magma is called lava. When thick lava cools, it becomes rock called **rhyolite**. Rhyolite is a light-colored, speckled rock that can be found across the United States and all around the world.

rhyolite

Thin Magma and Basalt

Some magma is thin and flows fast. When magma is thin, bubbles of steam escape easily. The volcano erupts more quickly. Steam and ash fly up, but there are few explosions. The thin lava flows from the crater and spreads far and wide.

Basalt is rock formed from thin lava flowing from "quiet" volcanoes. Basalt is dark and heavy. The Hawaiian Islands and much of the northwestern United States are made of basalt.

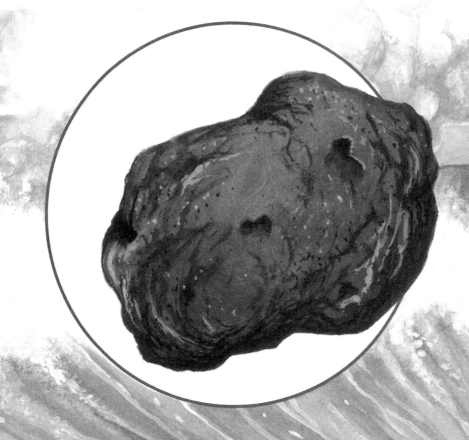

Obsidian: Glass From Volcanoes

Thousands of years ago people found mysterious chunks of black glass in the ground. When they broke the glass, they found that the pieces had curved sides and sharp edges—perfect for making knives and arrowheads.

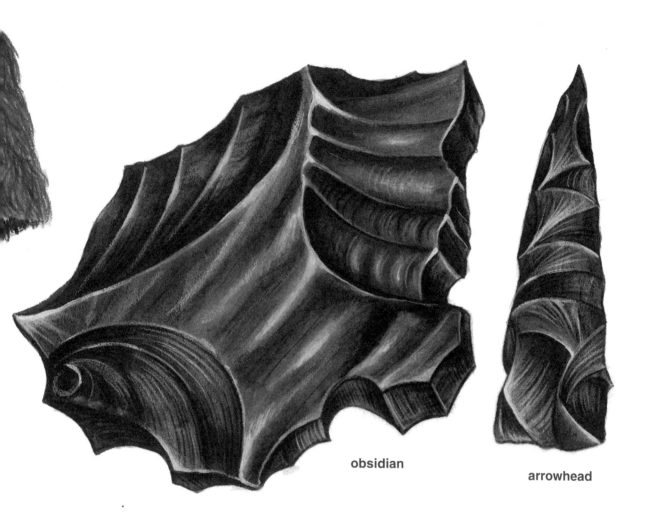

obsidian

arrowhead

Today this glass is called **obsidian** and we know that it comes from volcanoes.

Obsidian forms from thick lava that has lost most of its water. This makes it even thicker—too thick to form into rock in the usual way. It hardens into glass instead.

Famous Volcanoes

There are about 500 volcanoes around the world. And some of them are world-famous.

One of the oldest known is Mount Vulcano in Italy. The word "volcano" comes from its name. Another Italian volcano is Mount Vesuvius. It is famous because, almost 2,000 years ago, it buried an entire city—Pompeii—under 14 to 17 feet of ash and pumice.

In 1902 Mount Pelée erupted on the Caribbean island of Martinique. A huge cloud of steam and ash spilled down the mountainside. The temperature of that cloud was almost 1500°F. In minutes it set a nearby city on fire, sank 15 ships in the harbor, and killed 30,000 people.

plaster casts made from fossil remains of the people of Pompeii

Krakatoa

Krakatoa may be the most famous of all modern-day volcanoes.

It stood on an island in Asia lying between Java and Sumatra. In 1883 the volcano began to explode. The blasts were heard 3,000 miles away. The cloud of ash darkened the sky for more than 100 miles.

The great explosions raised huge waves that crossed the Indian Ocean and killed an estimated 36,000 people. When Krakatoa finished erupting, two thirds of the island had vanished.

The Sleeping Mountain

A year after Mount Saint Helens erupted, the land around it still looked bare and grim. But there were signs of life returning. Flowers sprouted by lakes still choked with ash and dead trees. Grasses grew and seedling trees sprang up. Scientists found the footprints of deer and they saw birds returning from the south.

How long will it take for the land to return to the way it was? Nobody knows for sure, just as nobody knows when—or if—the sleeping mountain will awaken again.